Hans Ed. Meyer

The Development of Writing

Alphabet Press

A Graphis Press Book
Published in the USA
by Alphabet Press, Natick, MA
ISBN 0-940032-06-6

10th printing

Der Unterricht im Schriftschreiben hat in der Ausbildung für alle Berufe der Gestaltung eine fundamentale Bedeutung.

Begabte Schüler erfassen den Sinn und entdecken das Geheimnis der geschriebenen Lettern. Das Schriftschreiben wird für sie zur Richtschnur; sie lernen den leeren Raum zwischen den Zeichen und Zeilen gleich wichtig zu nehmen wie die geschriebenen Formen. Sie lernen den Ablauf der Feder zu erlauschen und die Entwicklung der Schriftformen vom Kopf über den Arm in die Hand überzuleiten zum Seismographen, der Feder.

Der Schriftunterricht zeigt den Unterschied zwischen Ordnung und Chaos; er beweist die Wichtigkeit des kleinsten Details und führt ein in die Gesetze der Ordnung, die Grund sind zu jedem schöpferischen Tun, von der Architektur einer Kathedrale bis zum Inserat in der Tageszeitung.

Hans Meyer ist als einstiger Schüler Alfred Willimanns an der Kunstgewerbeschule Zürich der Lehrer dieses fundamentalen Faches. Wir sind ihm und seinem Verleger für das vorliegende sorgfältig gestaltete, wertvolle Handbuch dankbar. Es wird dazu beitragen, vielen das Geheimnis der geschriebenen Zeichen zu erschliessen.

Die Welt wird immer schneller und lauter. Die Einkehr zu Stillem und Anonymem tut not. Um Grosses leisten zu können, ist die Beherrschung des Kleinen und Kleinsten notwendig.

Hans Fischli, Direktor der Kunstgewerbeschule Zürich

In the training for any creative profession, the study of calligraphy can be of fundamental importance.

Talented pupils will realize the significance and meaning of the written letters, and for them, calligraphy becomes a guide. They learn that the space between the characters and the lines is as important as the characters themselves. They grow sensitive to the movement of the pen and are able to transfuse the image of the character that is in the head by way of the arm into the hand and so to the seismograph, the pen.

The study of calligraphy reveals that pressure demands counter-pressure, and one becomes aware of the difference between order and chaos. The science of calligraphy points to the importance of the smallest detail and introduces the laws of order that are the basis of all creative activity, from the architecture of a cathedral to an advertisement in a newspaper.

Hans Meyer, a former pupil of Alfred Willimann is now teacher of this fundamental subject at the School of Arts and Crafts in Zurich. We are grateful to him and his publisher that this concise and useful work can be made available to the many persons who wish to discover the secret of written characters.

The world becomes increasingly noisier and more restless. Silence and anonymity are needed. To fulfill great things, the mastery of the smallest things is necessary.

Hans Fischli, Director of the School of Arts and Crafts, Zurich

La calligraphie peut jouer un rôle fondamental dans la formation de tout créateur.

Les élèves sincères et doués se rendent comptent chaque jour de l'importance et de la signification des caractères écrits et, pour eux, la calligraphie prend sa vraie valeur. Ils comprennent vite que l'espace entre les lettres et les lignes est aussi important que les lettres elles-mêmes. Ils deviennent sensibles aux mouvements de la plume à laquelle ils sont bientôt capables de communiquer, par l'intermédiaire de leur bras et de leur main, l'image même du caractère qu'ils ont en tête.

L'étude de la calligraphie évoque la différence entre équilibre et chaos. Elle démontre l'importance des moindres détails et établit les lois du bon ordre régissant toute activité créatrice, qu'il s'agisse de l'architecture d'une cathédrale ou de la conception d'une annonce de presse.

Hans Meyer a étudié sous la direction d'Alfred Willimann et est maintenant professeur d'écriture à l'Ecole des arts et métiers de Zurich. Nous lui sommes reconnaissants, de même qu'à son éditeur, de cet ouvrage, dont la concision et la valeur se révèleront précieuses à tous ceux qui cherchent à pénétrer les secrets des caractères écrits.

Ce monde, toujours plus bruyant, toujours plus instable, a besoin de silence et d'anonymité. Pour accomplir de grandes choses, il faut d'abord apprendre à dominer les détails.

H. Fischli, Directeur de l'Ecole des arts et métiers, Zurich

Alle in diesem Buch wiedergegebenen Schriftbeispiele wurden vom Autor nach historischen Vorlagen neu geschrieben, wobei bewusst auf die sklavische Nachbildung zugunsten einer Typisierung verzichtet wurde, um die Entwicklung der Schriftformen klarer zu zeigen. Zur Ergänzung des Alphabets wurden jeweils die in der historischen Vorlage fehlenden Buchstaben hinzugeschrieben. Quellennachweis siehe letzte Seite.

All the examples of scripts given in this book have been rewritten by the author from historical models. His aim in so doing has been not merely to imitate but to underline what is essential and typical in order to illustrate more clearly the development of written letter forms. To complete the alphabet in each case the historical text has been taken as a model for the missing characters that have now been added. Sources are listed on the last page.

Tous les exemples d'écritures repris dans cet ouvrage ont été tracés par l'auteur à partir de modèles historiques. Ce faisant, son but n'a pas été une simple imitation, esclave du modèle, mais bien une mise en évidence de ce que ces modèles présentent d'essentiel et de typique pour illustrer plus clairement le développement des formes d'écriture. Dans chaque cas, il a ajouté les lettres qui n'apparaissaient pas dans le texte ayant servi de modèle. Les sources de référence sont citées à la dernière page.

Während die Schriftzeichen selbst ihre Bedeutung nie ändern, sind ihre Formen steter Wandlung unterworfen. Hauptanteil daran hat die Kurrentschrift, die, aus den Kapital- und Buchschriften entstehend, diese immer wieder beeinflusst und verändert. Dieselbe Schrift, zu verschiedenen Zeiten und in verschiedenen Ländern geschrieben, entwickelt sich so unterschiedlich, dass ihr gemeinsamer Ursprung kaum mehr ersichtlich ist. Die anfänglich unbewussten Formveränderungen und Ligaturen werden durch die Charaktere der die Schrift schnell Schreibenden bedingt. Aus der Endsumme all dieser Abweichungen kristallisiert sich dann die Schrift, die dem Kollektivcharakter eines Volkes entspricht.

Das Schreibgerät und das zu beschriftende Material sind ebenfalls von grosser Bedeutung, denn eine Schrift, mit dem Meissel in Stein gehauen, hat einen andern Formcharakter als eine mit der Feder auf Papier geschriebene Schrift. Auch die gezeichnete und dann geschnittene Druckschrift unterscheidet sich wesentlich von der geschriebenen Schrift, die ihr ursprünglich zum Vorbild diente.

Das Schriftbild, bestehend aus Buchstabeninnenräumen und Buchstabenzwischenräumen, ändert je nach der Federstellung seinen Duktus. Bei steiler Federstellung werden die Räume spitz und schmal (Kurrentschrift), bei horizontaler Stellung breitlaufend (Kapitalschrift).

Die einzelnen Zeilen sowie die ganzen Kolumnen, die als Linien und als Flächen wirken, sind in bestimmtem Verhältnis zur Fläche, auf der sie stehen. Sie gliedern die Fläche und schaffen neue Räume.

While letters do not alter in 'meaning', their forms are subject to continual change. Current hands are mainly responsible for this; themselves deriving from capitals and bookface types,they constantly influence and alter these. The same script, written at different times in different places, develops along quite different lines which little reveal a common origin. Such developments begin with unconscious formal mutations and ligatures prompted by the character of those who write the script at speed. The sum total of these small alterations makes up the collective character embodied in a national hand.

The tools and the material used in writing are major determinants of its form—letters that are chiselled in stone and those that are written with a pen on paper will develop different forms due to these different techniques; and the printed letter which is drawn and then cut, differs distinctly from the handwritten character that served originally as its model.

The 'pattern' created by the black lines of the letters and by the white spaces both within the individual letters and between them, alters according to the holding of the pen. A steeply slanting pen creates the sharp narrow forms of the running hand, while a pen held with a nearly horizontal nib makes for rounded, expansive capitals. Single lines and columns of lines having the effect of strips and rectangles are related to the format of the background that bears them; they divide its space and create whole new patterns of space.

Si la valeur phonétique des caractères écrits reste pratiquement invariable, leur forme évolue constamment. Les écritures courantes sont, pour une grande part, responsables de cette évolution; elles dérivent, à l'origine, des alphabets de lettres capitales et des écritures livresques, qu'elles ne cessent à leur tour d'influencer et d'altérer. L'évolution des caractères se fait dans le temps et dans l'espace et il est bien difficile, après un certain temps, d'en discerner l'origine commune. Le développement autonome commence par de simples mutations inconscientes et par des ligatures plus ou moins accentuées, dues uniquement à la personnalité du scribe. C'est l'ensemble de ces altérations, en elles insignifiantes, qui détermine les caractéristiques de l'écriture d'un peuple.

Les instruments utilisés et la matière sur laquelle est tracée l'écriture ne sont pas moins déterminants: les caractères, gravés dans la pierre ou tracés à la plume sur du papier, présenteront des formes différentes directement en rapport avec la technique adoptée. De même, la taille d'un caractère d'imprimerie diffère essentiellement du modèle écrit dont on s'est servi au départ.

Une écriture est déterminée par le rapport entre le tracé de l'outil (noir) et les parties blanches des contre-poinçons et des approches. Son aspect est variable suivant la position de la plume. Une position fortement inclinée donne une écriture aiguë et étroite (cursives); par contre, une position horizontale engendre des caractères larges et ronds (capitales).

Les lignes et les colonnes formant la structure d'une page sont dans un rapport précis avec l'ensemble de la surface où elles sont disposées. Elles la divisent et l'articulent de façon toujours nouvelle.

Zeitfolge der Schriften
Time sequence of scripts
Suite chronologique des écritures

Griechische Lapidarschrift
8.-5. Jh. v. Chr.
Greek Lapidary Writing
8th-5th century BC
Caractères lapidaires grecs
8e-5e s. av. J. C.

Römische Lapidarschrift 2. Jh. v. Chr
Roman Lapidary 2nd century BC
Caractères lapidaires
romains 2e s. av. J. C.

Rustika 4.-5. Jh.
Rustic Capitals 4th-5th cent.
Rustica 4e-5e siècle

Kapitalis Quadrata 1.-4. Jh.
Square Capitals 1nd- 4th cent.
Quadrata (majuscules) 1e-4e s.

Römische Unziale 4.-5. Jh.
Roman Uncial 4th-5th cent.
Onciale romaine 4e-5e s.

Altitalienische Schriften 4.-11. Jh.
Old Italian Scripts
4th-11th centuries
Anciennes écritures ita-
liennes 4e-11e siècle

Westgotische Schrift 10. Jh.
Visigothic Writing 10th cent.
Ecriture wisigothique 10e s.

Frühgotische Schrift 13. Jh.
Early Gothic Script 13th cent.
Ecriture gothique 13e siècle

Gotische Kursive 14.-15. Jh.
Gothic Cursive 14th-15th cent.
Cursive gothique 14e-15e s.

Gotische Schrift (Textur) 14.-15. Jh.
Gothic Script (Textura)
14th-15th centuries
Ecriture gothique (textura)
14e-15e siècle

Fraktur 16.-19. Jh.
Fraktur 16th-19th cent.
Caractères allemands
(Fraktur) 16e-19e siècle

Deutsche Spitzfederkurrent 16.-19.
German current hand
written with a sharp pen
16th-19th centuries
Ecriture allemande
tracée au moyen d'une plume
pointue 16e-19e siècle

Majuskel-Kursive 1.-2. Jh.
(ältere römische Kursive)
Majuscule-Cursive 1st-2nd cent.
(early Roman Cursive)
Cursive majuscule 1er-2e s.
(deuxième époque)

Minuskel-Kursive 3. Jh.   Römische Halbunziale 5. Jh.
(jüngere römische Kursive) _____ Roman Half-Uncials 5th cent.
Minuscule-Cursive   Semi-onciale romaine 5e s.
(Later Roman Cursive 3rd cent.)
Cursive minuscule 3e siècle
(troisième époque)

Merowingische Schrift 7.–8. Jh.   Irische und angelsächsische
Merovingian Script   Halbunziale 5.–12. Jh.
7th–8th centuries   Irish and Anglo-Saxon
Ecriture mérovingienne   Half-Uncial 5th–12th cent.
7e–8e siècle   Semi-onciale irlandaise
                                et anglo-saxonne 5e–12e s.

Karolingische Schrift 8.–12. Jh.
Carolingian Script
8th–12th centuries
Ecriture carolingienne
8e–12e siècle

ndgotisch (Rotunda) 15. Jh.   Humanistische Schrift 15. Jh.
tunda 15th century   Humanistic Script 15th cent.
nde gothique (Rotunda)   Ecriture humaniste 15e s.
  siècle

                       Klassizistische Schrift 18. Jh.
                       Classical Script 18th century
                       Ecriture classique 18e siècle

                       Lateinische Spitzfeder-
                       kurrent seit dem 18. Jh.
                       Latin current hand written
                       with a sharp pen since
                       the 18th century
                       Ecriture latine tracée au
                       moyen d'une plume pointue
                       à partir du 18e siècle

Die Schriften
der römischen Zeit

Der Ursprung der Schrift reicht weit zurück und ist unerforscht. Die römischen Schriftzeichen, mit denen unsere Schriftentwicklung beginnt, sind dem griechischen Alphabet entnommen. Die Zeilen der frühen griechischen Schrift sind abwechselnd von links nach rechts und von rechts nach links laufend.

The Letters
of the Roman Era

Although its origins are more distant and obscure, our writing may be said to start with the Greek alphabet from which the Roman letters that go to make up the alphabet used in the west today derive. The Greek scripts read from right to left and left to right alternatively.

Les styles de la
période romaine

Les origines exactes de l'alphabet restent indistinctes. Les caractères romains, qui sont à la base de notre alphabet actuel, s'apparentent aux caractères grecs lus, à l'origine, alternativement de droite à gauche et de gauche à droite.

Die ersten römischen Schriften sind, wie die griechischen, in Stein geritzt. Ihre Zeichen haben gleich starke Balken und sind ohne Seriven.

The first Roman scripts were, like the Greek ones, carved in stone. The strokes were of equal thickness; there was no shading and no serif.

Les premières écritures romaines, tout comme les caractères grecs, sont gravées dans la pierre. L'épaisseur des traits est constante, sans plein ni délié et sans empattement.

Später wird die Lapidarschrift (= Steinschrift) mit breitem Schreibgerät auf den Stein vorgeschrieben und nachgemeisselt. Auf diese Weise entstanden die Serive und die verschieden dicken Striche.

Later the lapidary (stone-engraved) letters were painted on the stone with a square-cut tool and then incised; from such means resulted the thick and thin variations of the strokes and the serifs.

Ultérieurement, les caractères lapidaires sont, avant la gravure, tracés sur la pierre au moyen d'un instrument à profil large; les pleins et les déliés, de même que les empattements, apparaissent simultanément.

echische Lapidarschrift 5. Jh. v. Chr.
teinischer Text in griechischer Schrift.)
eek Lapidary Writing 5th cent. BC
tin text in Greek writing)
iture lapidaire grecque 5e s. av. J. C.
xte latin en caractères grecs)

PΕΜΘΑ
ΟΤΑVΑΨΜ
ΟΔΙΟΥΧΜΕΝ
ΑΤΟΔΑΝΑΧΑΤ
ΙϘΕΤΙΜ
ΥΥΟΙΧΙΑ
ϘΕΜΔΟΜΕϷ
ΟΔΙΟΥΧϚΤΟΔ

nische Lapidarschrift 2. Jh. v. Chr.
nan Lapidary 2nd cent. BC
idaire romaine 2e s. av. J. C.

CORNELIVS·LVCI
VS·SCIPIC·BARBA
TVS·CNAIVOD·PA
RYFHQVGXKMZ

ische Lapidarschrift 1. Jh.
an Lapidary 1st cent.
daire romaine 1er siècle

MATRONIS·A
FLIABVS·M·M
ARIVS·KGCEH
DPQYXZJUVW

Die Entwicklung der geschriebenen Schrift beginnt mit der römischen Kapitalis (Capitalis Quadrata). Bei den ersten auf Papyrus oder Pergament geschriebenen Kapitalschriften wurde die Rohr- oder Kielfeder beinahe parallel zur Schreiblinie gehalten. Sie versuchten, die in Stein gemeisselten Buchstaben nachzuahmen.

The development of written letters begins with the Roman square capitals. The early scripts were written on vellum with an edged reed or quill nib held nearly parallel to the base line; they tried to copy the characteristics of letters incised in stone.

Toutes nos écritures dérivent de la «capitalis quadrata». Les premières écritures sont tracées sur papyrus au moyen du calame ou de la plume d'oie, avec une position presque horizontale. Elles tendent à imiter les capitales gravées dans la pierre.

In der Quadrata des 4. Jahrhunderts sind die Buchstaben teilweise vereinfacht. Das Bestreben nach schnellerem Schreiben wird sichtbar.

In the Roman square capitals of the 4th century, the characters were somewhat simplified. The desire to write faster made itself felt.

Dans la quadrata romaine du 4ème siècle, certaines lettres sont simplifiées. La tendance vers une forme d'écriture plus rapide se fait sentir.

Die Rustica ist eine mit stark schräger und bequemer, immer gleichbleibender Federhaltung geschriebene Kapitalis. Auch hier ist es das Bestreben nach schnellem Schreiben, das zu einem völlig neuen Schriftcharakter führt.

Rustic capitals were written with a square-edged pen held at a strong and constant slant with a nearly vertical nib. Once more it was the wish to write faster that led to a new hand.

La «capitalis rustica» est tracée avec une position de plume constante et fortement inclinée. Ici également la recherche d'une écriture plus rapide se traduit par l'apparition de formes tout à fait nouvelles.

Die Unziale besteht aus Buchstabenformen der Kapitalis und der Majuskel-Kursive. Die religiösen Werke der ersten Christen sind in dieser Schrift geschrieben.

Uncial letters took their forms from the square capitals and from written majuscules. The religious works of the early Christians were written in this hand.

Les formes de l'onciale sont inspirées de la capitalis et de la majuscule cursive. Les textes religieux des premiers chrétiens sont écrits dans ces caractères.

talis Quadrata 4. Jh.
an Capitals 1st cent.
tales romaines 1er siècle

ETPICTVMCRO
CEOVELAMEN
BDÇGKHQXYZS

talis Quadrata 4. Jh.
are Capitals 4th cent.
italis quadrata 4e siècle

ATQ·ILIVMINPR
AECEPSPRONOI
RA·BDFGHKXYZ·

tika 5. Jh.
tic Capitals 5th cent.
italis rustica 5e siècle

COEVMQVELAPETVM
QVECREAT·SAEVOMQ·
TYPHOEA·DKBÇNFIXZ

nische Unziale 5. Jh.
nan Uncials 5th cent.
iales romaines 5e siècle

TORRENTISqu
EMNONPERTR
ABCDFChKLXYZ

Während sich die Kapitalis zur Rustika und Unziale entwickelte, wandelte sie sich gleichzeitig zur Kurrentschrift. Die mit der spitzen Feder schnell und flüchtig geschriebenen, oder mit dem Stift in die Wachstafel geritzten Buchstabenformen vereinfachen sich und werden häufig zusammengehängt. Es entstehen Ligaturen und Ober- und Unterlängen und aus der Majuskel- bildet sich die Minuskel-Kursive. Diese Kleinbuchstabenschrift wird später massgebend für die weitere Entwicklung der abendländischen Schrift.

While the square capitals developed into the Rustica and Uncials, they also underwent development into a current style, written for daily use quickly and with little care, with pointed pen or stylus on papyrus or wax. The shapes of the letters were simplified and often joined, ascenders and descenders appeared —from the majuscule a minuscule-cursive was formed. These minuscules were to become decisive in the further development of western lettering.

Parallèlement au développement en rustica et en onciale, la quadrata donne naissance à une écriture courante, mieux adaptée à un usage quotidien et rapide, tracée à l'aide d'un style ou d'une plume pointue, sur papyrus ou tablette de cire. Les lettres sont jointes et leur forme est simplifiée; allongements du haut et du bas apparaissent et la majuscule donne naissance à une minuscule qui jouera un rôle décisif dans le développement des écritures occidentales.

In der Halb-Unziale sind die schreibflüchtigen Formen der Minuskel-Kursive zu einer regelmässig proportionierten Buchschrift gestaltet. Auch sie wurde, wie die Unziale, mit horizontaler Federhaltung geschrieben. Sie ist uns hauptsächlich aus den religiösen Werken der ersten Christen bekannt.

The quickly written letters of the minuscule-cursive took regular and proportioned shape as Half-Uncials. They were written, as the Uncials, with a reed or quill pen held with a nib parallel to the base line. The style is mainly known to us from the ecclesiastical works of the early Christian scribes.

Dans la semi-onciale, les formes rapides et précises de la minuscule cursive assument les proportions régulières des caractères en usage dans les livres. Elle aussi, comme l'onciale, est tracée selon une position horizontale de la plume. Ce style nous en a été transmis principalement par les manuscrits religieux des premiers chrétiens.

kel-Kursive 1. Jh.
scule-Cursive 1st cent.
ve majuscule 1er siècle
nière époque)

PRABERT·QVESVAECT
ACVLATRISTIAMORI
TISQVA·DFGHKNXYZ

kel-Kursive 2. Jh.
e römische Kursive)
cule-Cursive 2nd cent.
Roman Cursive)
ve majuscule 2e siècle
ième époque)

VS) FABVLLIVS MACER O-
CLASSIS PRAETOR(IAE)
NATIVM(TRIERE) TIG-
EMIT P... HKQVYZ

skel-Kursive 3. Jh.
ere römische Kursive)
scule-Cursive
Roman Cursive)
ve minuscule 3e siècle
sième époque)

nodum xysticor- | um et
licorum et- | juidem familiare
s) | praero gativas integras

sche Halbunziale 5. Jh.
n Half-Uncial 5th cent.
onciale romaine 5e siècle

a omne qu(od) | fit, antequam
t, non fuit, nos c | um fili...
rxy

Die Nationalschriften

Die römischen Schriften wurden von allen Ländern, die von Rom beherrscht waren, übernommen und auch nach dem Zerfall des römischen Reiches beibehalten. Die Kapitalis, Rustika, Unziale und Halb-Unziale ändern sich nicht; die Kursive aber, die schnell und täglich geschriebene Schrift, zeigt bald in jedem Land ihre besondere Eigenart.

In Italien entstand die päpstliche Kuriale, die römische Halbkursive, die altitalienische Bücherschrift und die langobardisch-beneventanische Schrift.

The National Hands

Roman scripts were adopted by all the areas under the rule of Rome, and were retained after the collapse of the Empire in the 5th century. The square capitals, Rustica, Uncial and Half-Uncial scripts did not alter, but the everyday, quickly written cursives soon developed individual character in the various areas.

In Italy there were developed the Papal Curial, the old Italian book-script and the Lombardic Beneventan scripts.

Les écritures nationales

L'écriture romaine est adoptée dans tout l'empire et se maintient après la période de déclin du 5ème siècle. La quadrata, l'onciale et la semi-onciale demeurent inaltérées mais les écritures coutantes prennent peu à peu un caractère individuel en rapport direct avec la région où elles se développent.

En Italie apparaissent à cette époque l'écriture des missives pontificales, l'ancienne écriture livresque italienne et l'écriture lombardo-bénéventine.

15

In Frankreich wandelte sich im 7. Jahrhundert die römische Kursive in die merowingische Schrift, aus der im 8. Jahrhundert, unter Karl dem Grossen, die karolingische Schrift hervorgeht.

In France the Roman cursive developed into the Merovingian script of the 7th century, and into the East-Frankish script of the 8th century. In the latter, the beginnings of the Carolingian letters can be seen.

En France, la cursive romaine donne naissance, au 7ème siècle, à l'écriture mérovingienne et, plus tard, à l'écriture carolingienne du 8ème siècle.

In Spanien entwickelte sich nach der Eroberung des Landes durch die Westgoten, die westgotische Schrift als Abart der merowingischen.

In Spain, after the conquest by the Visigoths, a style related to the Merovingian was developed as Visigothic writing.

Après la conquête de l'Espagne par les Wisigoths, la cursive romaine se transforme pour donner l'écriture wisigothique qui s'apparente à l'écriture mérovingienne.

ingische Bücherschrift 7. Jahrh.
ngian Book Script, 7th century
e mérovingienne 7e siècle

greges pascuntur | apastori-
c come | debatis et lanis ope-
| mini. Et quod crassum era(t)

ingische Diplomschrift.
. Jahrh.
ngian Document Script.
h century
e mérovingienne pour chartes
uments officiels. Moitié 8e

martyr ş(an)c(tu)s Bonefatius
| re requiescit, sup(er) fluvio
(er) hanc | D(e)o inspirante in-
videmur. Er– | go cognoscat
udo seu indust-

ingische Übergangsschrift.
. Jahrh.
ngian Transitional Script. End
century
e mérovingienne transitoire.
8e siècle

)s vero, q(ou)d fieri n(on) cre-
ego ipse | aut aliquis ex
– (us) meis v(e)l quili– | bet
ona hanc carta(m) traditionis

otische Schrift, 10. Jahrh.
hic script, 10th century
e wisigothique. 10e siècle

it. Nonnumqua(m) | heretici
c mira- | c(u)la faciunt, sed
ore | mia afflictionis sue abs-

Die Schrift der Iren und Angelsachsen ist nicht aus der römischen Kursive, sondern aus der römischen Halb-Unziale entstanden. Man unterscheidet zwei Hauptarten: eine durch horizontale Federhaltung breitlaufende, runde, die hauptsächlich in Irland geschrieben wurde, und eine mit schräger Federhaltung schnell geschriebene, schmale und spitze Halb-Unziale, die im Gebiet des heutigen England entstanden ist. Römische Missionare, die im 5. Jahrhundert das Christentum nach Irland und England brachten, haben diese Schrift dort eingeführt. Ihre religiösen Werke sind in der Halb-Unziale geschrieben.

The lettering of the Irish owed, not to the Roman cursive but to the Half-Uncial brought by missionaries of the Roman Church in the 5th century. The letters were written painstakingly with a horizontal nib. The conversion of what is now England to Christianity was brought about by Irish monks, and while this determined the shape of Anglo-Saxon writing, the Half-Uncial there developed a character of its own, being written with more speed and more slant of the pen with a resultant pointed effect.

L'écriture irlandaise ne se rattache pas à la cursive romaine, mais à la semi-onciale qu'utilisaient les missionaires de l'église romaine du 5ème siècle. En convertissant l'Angleterre au christianisme, les moines irlandais introduisent l'usage de la semi-onciale qui, si elle reste la base de l'écriture anglo-saxonne, n'en développe pas moins des caractéristiques locales déterminées par la recherche d'une écriture plus rapide et par la position plus inclinée de la plume.

ac et mundus p ipsum
factus ÷ et mundus eum
n cognouit· IN sua·rbn

PATER NOSTER qui
es in caelis sā ficæ
tur·nom· boçhkẋy

consideret·Et tunc illa
naturam quę super ip-
sam est·In ·bfghkxyz·

Usqui pghiunizentam Aeter
mtatir nobir aditum zleuica
monte referart· dphlquxyz æ

Die karolingische Schrift

Die karolingische oder fränkische Schrift ist unter dem Einfluss Karls des Grossen entstanden. Er war ein grosser Förderer des kulturellen und religiösen Lebens. Im Jahre 789 schrieb er die karolingische Schrift für alle Abschriften vor, da die schwer leserliche, mit Ligaturen und Abkürzungen überladene merowingische Schrift nicht mehr befriedigte.

Die karolingische Schrift entwickelte sich nur langsam. Im 8. Jahrhundert entstand eine Übergangsschrift, in der die Buchstabenformen einfacher und leserlicher wurden, die aber noch häufig merowingische Elemente aufwies. Erst im Laufe des 9. Jahrhunderts hat sie ihre eigene Form gefunden.

The Carolingean Writing

The Carolingian or Frankish script was developed under the influence of Charlemagne, who did much to further the religious and cultural life of his time. In 789 he decreed the use of Carolingian writing as a standard copying style to replace the national hands that had become largely illegible and corrupt.

The Carolingian Minuscule developed slowly. The 8th century script had many Merovingian elements, though the letters were simplified and made more legible. In the 9th century, the Carolingian writing found its own shape and character.

L'écriture carolingienne

L'écriture carolingienne ou franque apparaît sous l'influence de Charlemagne. Grand protecteur de la vie religieuse et culturelle, il en décréta l'usage officiel en 789, éliminant ainsi les différentes écritures nationales, d'ailleurs devenues pratiquement illisibles.

La minuscule carolingienne se développe lentement. Le 8ème siècle connaît une écriture transitoire où les formes des caractères sont simplifiées et gagnent en lisibilité. On y trouve encore fréquemment des éléments mérovingiens et c'est seulement au cours du 9ème siècle que la minuscule carolingienne trouve sa propre expression.

Als Versalien diente die Rustika; die ersten Zeilen der mit Initialen reichgeschmückten Buch- und Kapitelanfänge sowie die Titel und Auszeichnungen im Text, sind meistens mit der Kapitalis der Rustika oder der Unziale geschrieben. Die karolingische Schrift verbreitete sich rasch in allen Provinzen des fränkischen Reiches und verdrängte die Nationalschriften in Italien, Spanien und England.

Rustica was used for capital letters, and the first lines of chapters as well as titles and emphasised words were also in Rustica or in Uncials. The capitals and the new cursive text were both written with a pen nib slanted at the base line. Carolingian writing quickly spread and supplanted the several national hands.

Les majuscules sont tracées en rustica ou en onciale, de même que les titres et les premières lignes d'un chapitre. Majuscules et minuscules sont tracées à l'aide d'une plume inclinée. Cette nouvelle écriture se répand rapidement et finit par supplanter les différentes écritures nationales.

ngische Minuskel 8. Jh.
ngian Minuscule 8th cent.
scule carolingienne 8e siècle

Noli timere accipere mac
ricam con iugem tuam
Quod enim In ea nactum
eft. despū sco eft. bfhk qxȳ
ABCOEfcchij klMN
opqrstuxrryzyoco

ngische Majuskel 8. Jh.
ngian Majuscule 8th cent.
scule carolingienne 8e siècle

ngische Minuskel 9.–10. Jh.
ngian Minuscule 9th–10th cent.
scule carolingienne 9e–10e s.

que fint illa que cum
greca confentiant uen
tate deccina · bfhkpxyz
EPISTOLA HIE RONI
MI PRESBITERI AD
DAMASVM PAPAM
VRBIS · CECCKQXYZ

ngische Majuskel 9.–10. Jh.
ngian Majuscule 9th–10th cent.
scule carolingienne 9e–10e s.

alis der karolingischen Zeit
schmaler Feder konturiert)
al of the Carolingian Period
ne traced with a fine nib)
ale de la période carolingienne
ours tracés à la plume fine)

BENEDICATETC
VSTODIATVQS
FGHPKMLRXYZ

Im 12. Jahrhundert zeigte die karolingische Schrift bereits Züge, die auf die kommende gotische Schrift hinwiesen.

During the 12th century Carolingian writing showed signs of an evolving Gothic style.

L'écriture carolingienne évolue vers le style gothique, dont on trouve des traces dès le 12ème siècle.

ale der karolingischen Zeit
al of the Carolingian Period
ale de la période carolingienne

SCJENÒUCOTAB
FGÇKbPRLqCUX
qZ·ACEOFRSCNR

ale der karolingischen Zeit
schmaler Feder konturiert)
ine traced with a fine nib)
ale de la période carolingienne
ours tracés à la plume fine)

OCONIAERÇOJ
BOFKLSTUbp
qCUXYZOSY

le der späten karolingischen Zeit
chmaler Feder konturiert)
l of the late Carolingian Period
ine traced with a fine nib)
le de la fin de la période
ngienne (contours tracés à la
e fine)

HEC.ESTVERAK.
BDFGbIJLOHM
NOPQUTUXYZ

ngische Minuskel 11.–12 Jh.
ngian Minuscule 11th–12th cent.
cule carolingienne 11e–12e s.

Ego q̃s anno arguo & casti-
go. Emulare g& penitenn
angc.Ecc sto· bdfhkpxysz

ngische Majuskel 11.–12. Jh.
ngian Majuscule 11th–12th cent.
cule carolingienne 11e–12e s.

LIBRVAPOCALIPSIHE
DISSECOHSTAT·QVAM
VISEX·FCHKCOPYZMJ

Am Ende des 12. Jahrhunderts hat die karolingische Schrift typisch gotischen Charakter. Die Buchstaben sind mit steiler Federhaltung schmal und eckig geschrieben. Auch sie hat, wie die karolingische Schrift, ihren Ursprung in Frankreich, von wo aus sie sich bald in den benachbarten Ländern verbreitete.

At the end of the 12th century, Carolingian writing had a typically Gothic character. Written with an upright holding of the pen, the letters were narrow, condensed and angular. Both the Gothic and the Carolingian hands had their origins in France, and from there quickly spread to neighbouring countries.

A la fin du 12ème siècle, l'écriture carolingienne prend un caractère typiquement gothique. La position de la plume se rapproche de la verticale et les lettres deviennent étroites et anguleuses. Ces changements se manifestent d'abord en France, puis, comme pour l'écriture carolingienne, se propagent rapidement dans les pays environnants.

Die gotische Schrift

Zu Beginn des 13. Jahrhunderts, als auch in der Architektur der romanische Baustil vom gotischen verdrängt wurde, hat sich die frühe gotische Schrift endgültig gebildet.

Gothic Script

At the beginning of the 13th century, the Gothic letter was clearly formed and manifested the same need of the times for vertical stress that had replaced the round Roman arch by the pointed one.

L'écriture gothique

Dès le début du 13ème siècle, les lettres gothiques ont pris leur forme définitive. Comme dans le domaine de l'architecture, la tendance de l'époque vers la ligne verticale se fait sentir: l'ogive remplace le plein-cintre roman.

ingische Minuskel 12. Jh.
ingian Minuscule 12th cent.
scule carolingienne 12e siècle

ad'o comuiſſiſ. feralıſ exıtıı̈ alıq̃

remedıū quereuſ. p q̃o egre uı

té ab uuuuuctſl ma. hkryzs

ingische Majuskel 12. Jh.
ingian Majuscule 12th cent.
scule carolingienne 12e siècle

ABCDEFGHIJKLMHI
OPQRSTUVWXYℨ·H
1234567890

coℨ. Idem profecto ſuıntſe-

mēet nepotes. Meminıſ-

tıs credo. aghktqviwxyzs

ABCDEFGHIKLMN
OPQRSTUVWXYZ

Als sorgfältig geschriebene Buchschrift wird die frühgotische Schrift zur Textur (= Gitterwerk, Gewebe), eine Bezeichnung, die dem schmalen, engen, wie ein Gitterwerk wirkenden Schriftbild entspricht. Sie hat zuerst einfach gebrochene Buchstaben, in ihrer letzten Konsequenz aber sind sie doppelt gebrochen und ihre Formen sind, bis auf wenige Ausnahmen, durchwegs gerade und eckig.

Developed as formal book lettering, the early Gothic style of tall, narrow, black letters made with great precision and evenly spaced resembled a woven fabric, and was appropriately named Textura. At first, the style showed simple broken letters, but finally they were even doubly broken, and with a few exceptions all were upright.

Utilisés pour les textes officiels, les caractères gothiques se développent en longues et minces lettres noires, tracées avec soin et régulièrement espacées. L'ensemble rappelle curieusement la trame d'un tissu et prend fort justement le nom de textura. Les formes rondes ont pratiquement disparu.

Um die Mitte des 15. Jahrhunderts wird der Buchdruck mit beweglichen Lettern erfunden. Die ersten Druckbuchstaben werden vom Stempelschneider so genau wie möglich der geschriebenen Schrift nachgebildet. Die Textur wird damit zur ersten gesetzten und gedruckten Schrift.

About the middle of the 15th century book printing with movable types was invented. The forms of the type letters cut by a punch cutter aimed to resemble the manuscript letters of the time, so that Gothic Textura was used as a model.

Vers la moitié du 15ème siècle apparaissent les procédés d'imprimerie, avec caractères mobiles. Les premiers graveurs de caractères ont eu le souci d'imiter aussi exactement que possible les manuscrits de l'époque. Aussi la textura est-elle devenue le premier caractère d'imprimerie.

ur, Minuskel 15. Jh.
ura, Minuscule 15th cent.
ura, minuscule 15e siècle

Magnus dominus et
laudabilis nimus: in ci
vitas · fh kl p qr ſw x

ur, Majuskel 15. Jh.
ura, Majuscule 15th cent.
ura, majuscule 15e siècle

ABCDEFGHIJKLM
NOPQRSTUVWXYZ
ABCDEFGHIJKLNP
NRSTUVWXYZ

, Druckschrift 15. Jh.
a, Printed Type 15th cent.
a, caractère d'imprimerie 15e s.

oblationem seruitutis noſtre: ſz ꝗ
cūcte familie tue. Queſumus do
mine ut placatus accipias: dieſꝗ
nros i tua pace diſponas, atꝗ ab
eterna damnacióe nos eripi: et in
electoꝛ tuoꝛ iubeas grege mune
rari. Per xpm dm nrm Amen.

Die gotische Kursive ist die Weiterentwicklung der späten karolingischen Schrift, mehr oder weniger stark von der Textur beeinflusst.

Gothic cursive is the development of the late Carolingian script, sometimes more, sometimes less strongly influenced by Textura.

La cursive gothique, influencée par la textura, découle du dernier stade de l'écriture carolingienne.

So wie die römische Kursive die Kapitalschrift beeinflusste, so beeinflusst auch die gotische Kursive die Textur, die Kapitalschrift ihrer Zeit. Es entstehen Misch- oder Bastardschriften, die bald näher der Textur, bald näher der Kursive stehen.

Just as the Roman cursive influenced the Square Capitals, so the Gothic cursive made for changes in Textura. Mixtures arose, some of which were closer to Textura, others closer to the cursive.

Tout comme la cursive romaine modifia la quadrata, la cursive gothique transforme la textura. Ces transformations, appelées bâtardes, varient et donnent lieu à des mélanges qui se rapprochent plus ou moins de la cursive ou de la textura.

Auch die Bastardschriften werden vom Buchdruck übernommen. Die Schwabacher, der Kursive nahe verwandt, ist weitverbreitet und man findet sie noch heute in den Druckereien.

The mixture was also adopted by the book printer. Schwabacher type was very similar to the broad-pen cursive writing. It can still be found at printing presses today (1958).

Ces écritures bâtardes influencent également les caractères d'imprimerie. L'alphabet Schwabacher est, par exemple, très semblable à la cursive tracée à la plume épaisse; on l'utilise encore sporadiquement de nos jours.

sche Kursive 14. Jh.
ic Cursive 14th cent.
sive gothique 14e siècle

In zo taxen vnd ist in aynem ig-
lichen zaichen dritthalbe tax vnd
hat grossen gewallt in der Wag
Wenn es ist sein erhöhung vn

sche Urkundenschrift 14. Jh.
nic Document Script 14th cent.
ure gothique des actes 14e s.

Rebeack(er)e wid(er) kouffen
| len mit hund(er)t Marken Silb(er)s
vorgenanten gewi(c)htes so süllen …

die Rebeacke wid'kouffen wel-
ley. mit hundt marken silb'de
vorgenanten gewib tes so süllen

sche Kursive, Minuskel 15. Jh.
ic Cursive, Minuscule 15th cent.
sive gothique, minuscule 15e s.

genant Aristotiles der da was
Nicomachi sun von Macedom
vnd hat es gemacht seinem Jun
ger dem grassen chayser· fpktz

sche Kursive, Majuskel 15. Jh.
ic Cursive, Majuscule 15th cent.
ive gothique, majuscule 15e s.

ABCDEFFGHITKLOP
MNORGSTVWXYZ
1234567890

wabacher (Bastard) Druckschrift
h.
wabacher (Bastard) Printers' Type
cent.
habet Schwabacher (bâtarde)
siècle

vnd Mannlicher thaten, zur ewi-
gen gedechtnuß das Ritterspiel
der Thurnier, & bkmftzßoqryz!?
ABCDEFGHIJKLMNOP
QRSUVWXYZÄÖÜBCD
1234567890

Die Fraktur, eine andere Schriftart jener Zeit, hat auch die Kursive zur Grundlage, steht aber der Textur näher.

Fraktur, another type of the time also had the cursive as its basis, but was nearer to the Textura.

Les caractères dit gothiques on allemands sont une autre variante de la même époque; ils découlent également de la cursive mais se rapprochent davantage de la textura.

In Deutschland blieb die Fraktur bis ins 20. Jahrhundert die Buch- und Zeitungsschrift.

In Germany, Fraktur remained the common book and newspaper type until the 20th century.

En Allemagne, les caractères «gothiques» sont restés en usage jusqu'au 20ème siècle pour l'impression des livres et des journaux.

tur, Minuskel 16. Jh.
tur Minuscule 16th cent.
ctères allemands (fractur),
uscules 16e siècle

Do man zalt nach Chri-
sti Jesu vnnsers liebenn
herren · dfgjkpqlsvwxy

tur, Majuskel 16. Jh.
tur Majuscule 16th cent.
ctères allemands (fractur),
scules 16e siècle

ABCDEFGHIK
LMNOPQRST
VVWXYZ

ur, Druckschrift 16. Jh.
tur Type 16th cent.
ctères allemands (fractur)
primerie 16e siècle

Im Bernbiet, aber ich sage nicht
wo, liegt ein Bauernhof am son=
nigen Rain. Bei djkpqsvwxyz

ABCDEFGHJKLMN
OPQRSTUVWXYZ

1234567890

Genau so, wie die Architektur in Italien die Entwicklung zur reinen Gotik nie mitgemacht hat, hat auch die gotische Schrift dort nie gebrochene Formen angenommen; die Schriftformen blieben rund und breit und erhielten die Bezeichnung Rundgotisch oder Rotunda.

Just as architecture in Italy did not follow the full Gothic impulse, so Gothic lettering there was not carried to the final development of upright broken shapes, but remained instead round and broad, and was named Rotunda.

De même que l'architecture, en Italie, n'a jamais connu le gothique pur, l'écriture gothique y conserva des formes arrondies et larges; d'où son nom de ronde gothique ou «rotunda».

gotisch (Rotunda) Minuskel 15. Jh.
nda Minuscule 15th cent.
de gothique (Rotunda), minuscule
siècle

Mnipotens fem
piterne deus velp
bcfgbjklqwrxyz

gotisch (Rotunda) Majuskel 15. Jh.
nda Majuscule 15th cent.
le gothique, majuscule 15e s.

ABCDEFGHIK
LMNOPHRS
TUVWXYZ

otisch (Rotunda) Druckschrift

da Type 15th cent.
gothique, caractères d'imprimerie
cle

Gloria laudis refonet in ore
omniū Patri genitoqz proli
fpiritui fancto pariter Reful
tet laude perhenni Labori
bus dei vendunt nobis om

Die humanistische Schrift

In Italien erfährt die Schrift im 14. und 15. Jahrhundert, zur Zeit des Humanismus und der Renaissance, wieder eine grosse Wandlung. Das Studium der lateinischen Literatur, in der die Werke der antiken Dichter überliefert sind, macht die karolingische Schrift wieder bekannt. Die Humanisten ahmen sie beim Abschreiben dieser Werke nach und weil sie glauben, die Schrift der alten Römer zu schreiben, nennen sie sie die »antike Schrift« (Antiqua).

Da sich die gotische Schrift in Italien nie richtig durchzusetzen vermochte, fand die neue runde Schrift bald allgemeines Interesse und wurde in kurzer Zeit in ganz Italien geschrieben. (Die harte, gebrochene Schrift bezeichnete man, ebenso wie die Spitzbogenarchitektur, in herabwürdigendem Sinne mit dem Worte »gotisch«, womit barbarisch gemeint ist. Die Römer wurden vom 2.-5. Jahrhundert verschiedenemale von den Goten bedrängt und beherrscht und »gotisch« blieb deshalb die Bezeichnung für hart und barbarisch.)

Humanistic Script

In Italy, in the 14th and 15th centuries, writing once more underwent an important change. The Renaissance study of classical literature brought to light again the Carolingean minuscule in which, following Charlemagne's decree, the texts had been copied in the 9th to 11th centuries. The Humanists took the Carolingean writing as a model and, believing it to be the style of the ancients, named it Antiqua.

As the Gothic writing had never won full acceptance in Italy, the new round characters were of great interest and were soon generally adopted there. ('Gothic' was a term of depreciation. The Goths had from the 2nd to the 5th centuries fought the Romans several times and even conquered them. 'Gothic' for this reason implied all that was hard and barbarian, and so was applied to the hard broken writing of the North as to its vertical, pointed architecture.)

L'écriture humaniste

En Italie, l'écriture subit d'importants changements au cours des 14ème et 15ème siècles. La Renaissance ravive l'intérêt porté à la littérature classique et remet en lumière la minuscule carolingienne qui, après le décret de Charlemagne, était devenue l'écriture officielle aux 9ème et 10ème siècles. Les humanistes y voient le style des anciens et la prennent comme modèle en lui donnant le nom d'antiqua.

Les nouveaux caractères arrondis prennent rapidement le pas sur l'écriture, gothique qui n'avait jamais été très populaire en Italie. «Gothique» a en effet un sens plutôt péjoratif: du 2ème au 5ème siècle, les Goths sont les ennemis des Romains, leurs conquérants même. Le terme «gothique» évoque donc automatiquement le côté dur et barbare d'une chose et s'applique en particulier à l'écriture sévère et raide des Nordiques, de même qu'à leur architecture, où dominent la verticale et l'ogive.

Der Buchdruck, der jetzt die Herstellung der Bücher in grossen Mengen ermöglichte, verbreitete die humanistische Schrift in ganz Europa. Im 16. Jahrhundert verdrängt sie in allen lateinischen Ländern die gotischen Schriften. Wir verwenden noch heute Druckschriften, die im 16. und 17. Jahrhundert entstanden sind.

The printing of books, by making them available in large quantities, spread the humanistic style over Europe, and in the 16th century, it supplanted the Gothic in all Latin countries. We still use today types that originated in the 16th and 17th centuries.

Les progrès de l'imprimerie généralisent l'usage des livres et répandent le style humaniste à travers l'Europe. Dès le 16ème siècle, il a définitivement supplanté le gothique dans les pays latins. Nous utilisons encore de nos jours un alphabet connu soul le nom d'elzévir et dont l'origine remonte aux 16ème et 17ème siècles.

nistische Minuskel 15. Jh.
nistic Script Minuscule 15th cent.
scule humaniste 15e siècle

Superis habeo gratiam
quorum maiestate sug
gerente mihi fauorum
opperfici· djksvwxyzi

nistische Majuskel 15. Jh.
nistic Script Majuscule 15th cent.
cule humaniste 15e siècle

ABSOLVI·TANDE^M
ALIQVANO·DELE-
GATVM·MIHI·ABS
TE·CFJKPRUWXYz

istische Druckschrift 15. Jh.
istic Type 15th cent.
ères d'imprimerie humanistes
cle

Sic splendente domo, claris na-
talibus orta Scintillas, raraque
tuos virtu & ffghjkwxyz œæ?
RARAQUE TUOS VIR-
TUTE PARENTES ILLU
FGKHW JXMYDBNCIZ
1234567890

Die Kursive der humanistischen Schrift ist wieder die Folge rascher Schreib-
weise. Sie ist in den Kanzleien entstanden und trägt deshalb den Namen Can-
cellaresca. Bald wird sie überall geschrieben und sie verbreitet sich rasch in
den Ländern, die durch den Handel mit Italien in Berührung kommen. Sie wird
die allgemeine Kurrentschrift des Abendlandes, und unsere heutige Handschrift ist auf diese Kursive zurückzuführen.

The Humanistic cursive was, as other cursives, the result of fast writing. Be-
cause of its first use in official circles it was given the name of Chancery Cursive, and soon it was widely used, being spread by way of commerce to all countries in contact with Italy. The Chancery script became the current hand of
the west, and our handwriting today derives from it.

La cursive humaniste résulte d'un mode d'écrire plus rapide. Ayant vu le jour
dans les chancelleries d'Italie, elle porte le nom de cursive des chancelleries
et gagne rapidement les pays étrangers entretenant avec l'Italie des relations
commerciales. Elle devient progressivement l'écriture courante de l'Occident
et notre écriture actuelle en découle.

HVmanißimo Cofseruan
dißimo S.mio, Zra tutti gli de
uoti serui di .V.RZ. Sig. Ves
pasiano Xm phyareo Feraresc
Minoritano Con-chkqvwxz

& Culphum cü aliquo nau
igio armato, exceptis auro
et arge to: sub pena perden
di totü. quod fuit & kvwyz

ABCDEEFGHIJKLM
NOPQRSTUVWXYZ
ABCDEFGHIJKLM
NOPQRSTUVWXYZ

Die Kursive des 16. und 17. Jahrhunderts hat weichere und fliessendere Formen als jene des 15. Jahrhunderts. Sie wird in dieser letzten Form vom Buchdruck übernommen und zur Druckschrift gestaltet.

The cursive of the 16th and 17th centuries had more round and flowing forms than those of the 15th century. It was in this last form that it was developed as a printing type.

La cursive des 16ème et 17ème siècles présente des formes plus souples et plus coulantes. C'est à partir de ces formes que seront élaborés les caractères d'imprimerie.

manistische Kursive, Minuskel 16. Jh.
anistic Cursive Minuscule 16th cent.
ive humaniste, minuscule 16e s.

Anno con re detto di sopra no-
sopra Carta di S. M. remetten-
dosi questa Regia Camera nel-
uno, e nell'altro · bfhhjk vuxyz

manistische Kursive, Majuskel 16. Jh.
anistic Cursive Majuscule 16th cent.
ve humaniste, majuscule 16e s.

AABBB(CDDEEFFG
GHHIJKLMMMNN
OPPQQRRRJSTTU
VYYWWXXYYZ
ABCDEFGHIJKLNP
MORQUSTVWXYZ
1234567890

manistische Kursive,
schrift 16. Jh.
nistic Type 16th cent.
tères d'imprimerie humanistes
ècle

Syllanæ veteres urbis celebran-
tia cunas, Illustresque viros, to-
tamque & dfflfighjklmpßwxyz
NOBILIS UT FULUO DE-
CORATUR GEMMAM
KGPQWMXHJYNZÆŒ
1234567890

Die klassizistische Schrift

Im 17. Jahrhundert entsteht aus der humanistischen die klassizistische Schrift. Mitbestimmend an ihrer Form ist der Kupferstich, der in dieser Zeit die höchste technische Vollendung erreicht und die feinsten Linien zu reproduzieren vermag. Der Buchdruck ahmte auch diese Schriftart nach. Von Schriftschöpfern aus jener Zeit — Bodoni, Didot, Walbaum und andern — kennen wir Schriften, die noch heute zu den schönsten zählen.

The Classical Script

The Classical writing of the 17th century derived from Humanistic script but was shaped by the influence of copper-engraving which at the time reached its highest technical performance, reproducing the finest of lines. Book printing also aped the resultant style of heavy strokes and contrasting hair-lines, though it was not suited to relief printing. However, some of the types that were fashioned by this influence—Bodoni, Didot, Walbaum and others—still rank among the most beautiful.

L'écriture classique

L'écriture du 17ème siècle dérive de la cursive humaniste. Elle est cependant transformée par la technique de la gravure sur cuivre qui permet de reproduire des traits d'une extrême finesse. Les caractères d'imprimerie suivent la même voie et il en résulte un style fondé sur le contraste des pleins et des déliés. Ce style, peu conforme aux besoins de l'imprimerie, n'en a pas moins donné naissance à des alphabets que l'on continue à considérer parmi les plus beaux: Bodoni, Dédot, Walbaum, etc.

ssizistische Minuskel 18. Jh.
ssical Minuscule 18th cent.
uscule classique 18e siècle

Lycurgus ille legislato
cum conaretur cives fu-
os a moribus præsenti-
bus ad tem·fhjkqwxz

ssizistische Majuskel 18. Jh.
ssical Majuscule 18th cent.
uscule classique 18e siècle

LYCVRGVS ILLE LE
GISLATOR·CVMCO
NARETVR CIVES
BDFHJKPQXUWZ

sizistische Druckschrift 18. Jh.
ssical Type 18th cent.
actères d'imprimerie classiques
siècle

C'est à lui selon toute apparence,
que fait allusion un passage sou-
vent cité & dxfffifflhwkymbzææ
CHEF-D'ŒVRE DE L'ARTTY-
POGRAPHIQUE COMME LE
PREMIER ÆZBYJXKNWS
1234567890

zistische Kursive, Minuskel 18. Jh.
ical Italic Minuscule 18th cent.
cule italique classique 18e s.

Multi concionatores in
natura sua, licet occulte
superbi sunt, et multun
innitur· dfghjqkvwxyz

izistische Kursive, Majuskel 18. Jh.
sical Italic Majuscule 18th cent.
scule italique classique 18e s.

DARE SALVTEM E
COMIS ESSE ETIA
LIBERARE PERI-
FGHJKNUWXYZI

sizistische Kursive,
kschrift 18. Jh
sical Italic Type 18th cent.
que classique, caractères
primerie 18e siècle.

L'art admirable de l'imprimerie
a été inventé d'abord en Allemagne, à May   & fghjkopqusvwxyz
CELA ARRIVA   ENVIRON
L'AN 1440, ET, DEPUIS CE
BTFGWHJKMQVXYZ ÆŒ
1234567890

Die klassizistische Kursive wird unter dem Einfluss der Kupferstichtechnik zur Spitzfederkurrent. Schreibmeister jener Zeit haben sie zur höchsten Vollendung gebracht und sie ist heute noch Vorbild unserer Handschrift.

Under the influence of copperplate-engraving the Classical cursive writing developed into the pointed-pen current hand. Writing-masters of the time developed it to the highest perfection, and the style remains one model for our handwriting today.

Sous l'influence de la technique de la gravure sur cuivre, la cursive classique se transforme en une écriture courante tracée à la plume pointue. La perfection atteinte par les calligraphes de l'époque donne naissance au style «calligraphique», qui reste le modèle idéal de nos écritures contemporaines.

zfederkurrent 18. Jh.
ted Pen Current 18th cent.
ure courante à la plume 18es.

abcdefghijklmnopqrrstuvwxyzz

ABCDEFGHIJKLM

NOPQRSTUVWXYZ

1234567890

zfederkurrent 18. Jh.
ted Pen Current 18th cent.
ure courante à la plume 18e s.

La chiarizza del sangue accom-

pagnato da bbffff bjkgvfnwxyz

ABCDEEFGHIJK

LLMMNOPQRS

TUVWXYZXWV

1234567890

federkurrent, Fantasieschrift
n.(Gravour)
ted Pen Current 18th cent.
aved script
ure courante à la plume, style
sisiste 18e s., procédé de gravure

Philippus Roy de Macedoine avois fait

demolir et razer la ville d'Olynt Le Mais

Die moderne Schrift

Die Druckschrift, die sich anfangs bemühte, der geschriebenen Schrift mög-
lichst nahe zu kommen, hat bereits in der klassizistischen Zeit Ansätze zu eige-
ner Form. Im 19. Jahrhundert weicht sie mit dem Schriftbild der Egyptienne und
Grotesk endgültig von der federgerechten Form ab. Beide, Egyptienne und Grotesk, gehören zur Antiqua.

Modern types

Printing type, which at the beginning often imitated handwriting already showed
in the Classicist time tendencies to evolve independent character. In the 19th
century, with the appearance of the Egyptian (slab-serif) and Grotesque (sans-
serif), printers' types definitely leave handwritten shapes. Both Egyptian and
Grotesque are related to Antiqua.

L'écriture moderne

Les caractères d'imprimerie qui n'ont fait, d'abord, qu'imiter les caractères
manuscrits, tendent, dès la période classique, à poursuivre séparément leur
évolution. Au 19ème siècle, avec l'égyptienne et le bâton (désigné aussi sous
le nom d'antique), ils abandonnent définitivement leurs modèles manuscrits.
Tous deux se rattachent à l'antiqua.

Zu Beginn des 20. Jahrhunderts entstand eine Tendenz, die schematisierte,
in geometrischen Formen erstarrte Schrift aufzugeben, zugunsten humaneren,
dynamischeren Formen, die charakteristisch für die humanistischen Druckschriften der Renaissance sind. Diese, vom Autor dieses Büchleins entworfene
Schrift (Syntax-Antiqua), ist ein Beitrag, die moderne Druckschrift aus ihrer
festgefahrenen Erstarrung zu befreien.

At the beginning of the twentieth century there arose a tendency to reject
calligraphic scripts which were schematized and frozen in geometric rigidity
in favour of humaner, more dynamic forms which are characteristic of the
humanistic typescripts of the renaissance. The script in this small book
(Syntax-Antiqua), designed by the author, plays a contributory role in liberating
modern typescript from its restrictions.

Le début de notre siècle a vu s'affirmer une tendance à délaisser les caractères
d'imprimerie schématisés, figés dans des formes géométriques, au profit de
formes plus humains, plus dynamiques, telles que les ont incarnées les
Humanes de la Renaissance. Ce style de caractères conçu par l'auteur de cet
opuscule (Syntax-Antiqua) est une importante contribution à l'assouplissement
des caractères d'imprimerie modernes figés dans la routine.

nne, Mitte 19. Jh.
n, Mid 19th cent.
nne, moitié du 19e s.

Ancien imprimeur et ou-
vrier en lettres, graveur
de planc & bhjkqfwxyz!?
ANCIEN IMPRIMEUR
ET OUVRIER EN LET-
BDFGHJXKQSWZY Œ
1234567890

k Ende 19. Jh.
que, End of 19th cent.
e, fin du 19e s.

Den Grundstein für die Ste-
reotypie legte Goldschmied
William Ged & bkjqvwxyz!?
DEN GRUNDSTEIN FÜR
DIE STEREOTYPIE LEG-
TE ABVCHJWKMQZ ÆŒ
1234567890

Während die Schriftzeichen ihre
Bedeutung nie ändern, sind de-
ren Formen steter · bkpqvwxyz
WANDLUNG UNTERWORFEN
HAUPTANTEIL DARAN HAT DIE
KURRENTSCHRIFT · JMQVXYZ
1234567890

Bibliographie Bibliography	Prof. Dr. F. Steffens; Lateinische Paläographie, Bände 1, 2, 3 und Supplement Universitäts-Buchhandlung, Freiburg (Schweiz). 1904 Hermann Degering; Die Schrift, Verlag Ernst Wasmuth AG., Berlin. 1939 J. Mallon, R. Marichal, C. Perrat: L'écriture latine de la capitale romaine à la minuscule. Arts et métiers graphiques, Paris. 1939 Edward Johnston: Schreibschrift, Zierschrift und angewandte Schrift. Verlag Klinkhardt und Biermann, Leipzig. 1921 Kurt Siebert: Meisterbuch deutscher Schrift. Verlag für Kunstwissenschaft, Berlin. Jan Tschichold: Gute Schriftformen. Allg. Gewerbeschule Basel, Lehrmittelverlag des Erziehungs-Departements, Basel-Stadt. 1942 Peter Jessen: Meister der Schreibkunst aus drei Jahrhunderten. Julius Hoffmann Verlag, Stuttgart. 1923

Die Schriftbeispiele sind folgenden Werken entnommen:

The examples in this book are derived from the following sources:

Les exemples d'écritures reproduits ont été extraits des ouvrages suivants :

No 1, 2, 3	Degering, Die Schrift, S. 1, 4, 13
No 4, 7	Steffens, Lateinische Paläographie, S. 10, 15
No 5, 6	Degering, Die Schrift, S. 19, 29
No 8	Degering, Die Schrift, S. 7
No 9, 11	Steffens, Lateinische Paläographie (Band 1), S. 9, 17
No 10	L'écriture latine, T. 22
No 12	L'écriture latine, T. 25
No 13, 15	Steffens, Lateinische Paläographie (Band 1 und 2), S. 23, 62
No 14	Steffens, Lateinische Paläographie (Supplement), S. 24
No 16	L'écriture latine, S. 45
No 17	Steffens, Lateinische Paläographie (Supplement), S. 19
No 18, 19	Steffens, Lateinische Paläographie (Band 2), S. 40, 54
No 20	Steffens, Lateinische Paläographie (Band 2), S. 42
No 21	Johnston, Schreibschrift, T. 7
No 22	Biblioteca Vaticana. Serie C: Scritt. latine Nr. 6
No 23	Degering, Die Schrift, S. 40
No 24	Steffens, Lateinische Paläographie (Band 2), S. 36
No 25	Biblioteca Vaticana. Serie C: Scritt. latine. Nr. 11
No 26	Degering, Die Schrift, S. 61
No 29, 31	Degering, Die Schrift, S. 48, 63
No 30	L'écriture latine, S. 39
No 32, 33	Degering, Die Schrift, S. 69
No 34–37	Steffens, Lateinische Paläographie (Band 2), S. 70, 101
No 38–40	Siebert, Meisterbuch, S. 10, 19
No 41	Degering, Die Schrift, S. 104
No 42	Gute Schriftformen, (Heft 4), S. 2
No 43/44	Siebert, Meisterbuch, S. 5
No 45	Nürnberger Schwabacher, Haas'sche Schriftgiesserei AG, Münchenstein, Schweiz
No 46, 47	Siebert, Meisterbuch, S. 46
No 48	Walbaum-Fraktur, Schriftgiesserei H. Berthold AG., Berlin
No 49, 50	Degering, Die Schrift, S. 120
No 51	Reproduktion aus: Prof. Dr. E. Voulliéme, Die deutschen Drucker des 15. Jahrh., Druck und Verlag der Reichsdruckerei, Berlin 1922
No 52, 53	Johnston, Schreibschrift, T. 18
No 54	Garamond, Fonderie Deberny & Peignot, Paris.
No 55	Jessen, Meister der Schreibkunst, S. 97
No 56, 57	Gute Schriftformen (Heft 4), S. 15
No 58, 59	Degering, Die Schrift, S. 188
No 60	Satzschrift, Garamond-Kursiv, Fonderie Deberny & Peignot, Paris
No 61, 62	Steffens, Lateinische Paläographie (Supplement), S. 47
No 63	Bodoni, Bauersche Giesserei, Frankfurt am Main
No 64, 65	Degering, Die Schrift, S. 203
No 66	Bodoni-Kursiv, Bauersche Giesserei, Frankfurt am Main
No 67, 68	Degering, Die Schrift, S. 198, 199
No 69	Jessen, Meister der Schreibkunst, S. 166
No 70	Clarendon, Haas'sche Schriftgiesserei, Münchenstein, Schweiz
No 71	Schelter-Grotesk, Schriftgiesserei Schelter & Giesecke, Leipzig